# SITTINGBOURNE
## AND DISTRICT
### A Pictorial History

Lloyd's Mill, Sittingbourne, *c*.1916.

# SITTINGBOURNE AND DISTRICT

## A Pictorial History

Alan Cordell,
Bill Lee
and
Margaret Lee

Phillimore

1989.

Published by
PHILLIMORE & CO. LTD.
Shopwyke Hall, Chichester, Sussex



ISBN 0 85033 713 5

Printed and bound in Great Britain by
BIDDLES LTD.
Guildford, Surrey

## *List of Illustrations*

The illustrations appear by kind permission of the following: Mrs. Barden, 149; Mr. & Mrs. Baum, 16; A. S. Bennett, 170; Mr. P. Birch, 3; Mr. L. Boakes, 95, 138; Mr. K. Chisman, 71, 77, 131, 142; Mrs. G. Clark, 112; Mr. R. Cockell, 13, 28, 97; Mrs. B. Cornelius, 7, 20, 21, 137; Mr. Dane, 8; Mrs. Daw, 104; C. Dolding, 160; Mrs. N. Drake, 39, 136; Mr. B. Earl, 128; G. Faint, 151; Miss M. Forster, 127; Mrs. P. Foster, 111; Mrs. Gregory, 132; Mrs. Harrison, 93; Mrs. I. Hayler, 102, 103; Mrs. J. High, 30, 31, 32, 130; Mrs. M. Horsford, 35, 101; Mrs. Howard, 81; Mr. C. Jones, 96; Mr. S. Leaney, 5; L. Lukehurst, 173; W. Marsh, 154; Mrs. C. Mason, 10; Mrs. V. Mills, 34, 92; E. Pearce, 161, 162, 163; Mrs. Pilcher, 108; Mrs. K. Pope, 36, 87, 109; Mr. D. Pope, 24; T. Redshaw, 167; Mrs. E. Smith, 29; Mrs. B. Sidders, 4, 22; Mrs. L. Spree, 145; Mr. M. Stone, 1, 12, 23; Mrs. Turk, 150; Mr. Wakelen, 147; F. G. Willmott, 164, 166; Mrs Wright, 70, 153.

*Acknowledgements*

The authors offer their grateful thanks to the following: all contributors of pictures, who are acknowledged separately where possible; Karen Garton for her excellent typing; the staff of the *East Kent Gazette* and Sittingbourne Library for allowing easy access to their records; Nautical Pictorial for providing the historical information about postcards; Leslie Strevens for his contribution on Milton Creek. The authors also acknowledge the good work of those well-known Sittingbourne professional photographers of an earlier era – Ferris, Ramell and Wrigglesworth; they and their cameras have made a telling contribution to this book.

## *Introduction*

Sittingbourne, in north Kent, is a town of medium size situated on the original main road (the Roman Watling Street) from London to Dover, 40 miles east of the capital. Milton Regis and Murston are smaller adjoining districts which were for many years united with Sittingbourne in one Urban District Council.

Until medieval times, Sittingbourne was a tiny and little-known village. However, the murder of Archbishop Thomas à Becket at Canterbury in 1170 led to recognition and growth for Sittingbourne because it provided a convenient stopping stage for the thousands of Canterbury pilgrims who passed through each year on their way to the Becket shrine.

English monarchs also enjoyed the hospitality of Sittingbourne. King Henry V, on his triumphant return from the Battle of Agincourt in 1415, was entertained by John Northwood at the *Red Lion*. The present public house on the site, parts of which may be original, is called the *Lion*, but displays red lion sculptures. It is rumoured that the Red Lion name will be restored soon. George I and George II, on their way through Sittingbourne from the Continent, generally rested at a house belonging to the well-known local Lushington family. The *Red Lion* was in fact mentioned by the historian Hasted when he compiled his survey of Kent in 1778-99. Hasted went further and described the nearby *Rose Inn* as 'the most superb of any throughout the kingdom'. The *Rose* building has since been converted into a parade of shops, one of which is Woolworth's. In more recent times, the *Bull*, with its central position and attractive frontage, has become the town's best-known inn. The business brought by stage-coaches stimulated the expansion of Sittingbourne. However, a subsequent and even more powerful aid to development and prosperity was the suitability of the district for industry, as will be described later.

A final contribution to the town's growth has been the comparatively recent practice of many London business folk commuting long distances to work. Although 40 miles away, Sittingbourne has a fast and frequent rail service to and from London. Thus it has become a popular 'dormitory' town for workers in the capital, offering them close proximity to the attractive Kent coast and countryside, together with relatively easy daily business travel. For all these reasons, the population of the town has increased ten-fold over the last 100 years.

Milton Regis, to the north-west of Sittingbourne, was at one time the larger town. In fact, it was only overtaken by Sittingbourne in population around the middle of the last century. The original town stood where the parish church (Holy Trinity) is now, but it was plundered by the Danes under Hasten in 893 and then burnt by Earl Godwin's men in 1052. This site was liable to flooding from the nearby tidal creek so, when rebuilt, the new town was positioned on the higher ground close to Sittingbourne, at the head of the creek. The early prosperity of Milton Regis stemmed mainly from this waterway, now called Milton Creek. The town became a busy centre for water-borne trade, and was the home port for a large oyster fleet. In fact, 'Buy My Fine Milton Oysters' was one of the cries of London.

The village of Murston, to the north-east of Sittingbourne, was the last of the three settlements to develop. Rapid growth was brought about by the birth of the local brick and cement manufacturing industries around the middle of the last century, the biggest firm, Smeed Dean, being located at Murston. Undoubtedly these industries needed good water communications, and the choice of Murston as a site was influenced by its position half-way down Milton Creek on the east bank. The Creek, therefore, made a large contribution to the growth of Sittingbourne, Milton Regis and Murston, which now have a combined population of about 50,000.

The enormous numbers of houses built in the last 40 years have virtually filled in the farmland which used to separate the three settlements from the neighbouring villages of Bapchild, Tunstall, Borden and Kemsley, so these four places can now be considered as part of Sittingbourne and District.

**Milton Creek and Industry**

Milton Creek was originally the estuary of a small stream which rose in the vicinity of Bredgar and followed the valley that passes south-east of Borden and thence through Ufton Lane and Cockleshell Walk to Milton Regis. Between Bredgar and Borden, in the vicinity of Wren's Farm, is Hart's Delight (now wrongly spelt Heart's Delight), which in the Middle Ages was undoubtedly a watering place for wild animals. Up until quite recently it was possible after heavy rain to see water flowing down the bed of the original stream through Cockleshell Walk. A smaller stream, the Periwinkle, rose at Chalkwell and joined the main stream at Milton Regis and the two streams broadened out to form Milton Creek. A third stream, the Bourne, ran down Crown Quay Lane and entered the Creek further to the east. It is said that Sittingbourne derived its name from the Canterbury pilgrims who sat on the slope by the Bourne Stream to refresh themselves before the final stage of the journey to Canterbury. Wealthier pilgrims stayed at Milton which was later honoured by the addition of the suffix 'Regis'.

The Creek later became an important centre for the oyster fleets that worked in the Swale. Cockleshell Walk no doubt derived its name from this trade and the bed of the old stream which bordered it was only filled in a few years ago, when the road was widened and the new one-way traffic system introduced. By then the stream was nothing more than a rubbish dump. After widening, Cockleshell Walk became the west end of St Michael's Road.

The streams were, in fact, doomed much earlier, when the paper mills were constructed in the mid-19th century – the demand for water in paper making is considerable. The natural flow of water soon became inadequate and the paper mills (then Edward Lloyd Ltd., later Bowater, and now U.K. Paper) began sinking wells to supply their demands. The paper mills grew, but Milton Creek was robbed of its natural flow of pure water and the descent into the polluted, mud-silted waterway it later became had begun.

However, the Creek derived a new commercial importance as a centre of the thriving stock brick manufacturing trade and also of the cement industry. The banks of the Creek, from its head to the Swale, were lined on both sides by brick manufacturers. Among the better-known names were Smeed Dean Ltd., Chas. Burley Ltd., and Wills and Packham Ltd. Of these, Smeed Dean at Murston were by far the largest, ranking second only in the country to the London Brick Company in size. The reason for the proliferation of brick and cement manufacturers was that there was an almost inexhaustible supply of the chief raw materials in and around the Sittingbourne area, namely clay and chalk. Whilst the district provided the raw materials, the Creek provided the means of transporting the finished goods. The 'work horse' was the Thames spritsail sailing barge. All the main brick manufacturers had their own fleets of these vessels and many had their own yards for construction, repair and maintenance. Again Smeed Dean Ltd. was the largest, owning or operating about 80 craft at their peak. There were also independent barge yards which built and serviced vessels for those who did not have their own facilities. Most of these were situated near the head of the Creek.

With the advent of rail and road transport, the Thames barge ceased to be the main means of conveyance and by the outbreak of the Second World War these barges were virtually obsolete. Today, vessels are rarely seen on Milton Creek, though a single motor barge carries aggregate to the old Eastwoods wharf for concrete pipe manufacture.

Following the General Strike and the depression of the later 1920s, the brick trade declined and the smaller manufacturers soon disappeared. A.P.C.M., Wills and Packham, and Chas. Burley remained, and indeed continued to make bricks throughout the Second World War. In 1927 Smeed Dean changed hands and was later acquired by A.P.C.M., now Blue Circle, who recently shut the cement works but remain as the only brick manufacturer in the town. As a result of the sale of Smeed Dean Ltd., two former directors, George Andrews and his son Harold, were left with a small fleet of about six barges with no home base. They sought suitable alternative premises with the idea of building up a fleet of some 20-25 vessels and operating as general freight contractors. They found what they were looking for in the virtually bankrupt independent boat and barge yard near the head of Milton Creek, at that time known as the Sittingbourne Shipbuilding Co. Ltd. and occupying the former White's yard. Harold Andrews acquired the business in 1930. Another former Smeed Dean official, Sid Ellis, also brought in some barges and, although there was no legal partnership, all barges wore the same bob and were known as belonging to Ellis and Andrews.

On acquiring the Sittingbourne Shipbuilding Company, Mr. Andrews retained the services of the founder of the Company, Mr. H. W. Harvey, an independent marine surveyor, as technical advisor. He also brought in, from Smeed Dean Ltd., Vic Horsford, then foreman shipwright, together with several members of his gang. During the 1930s, '40s and early '50s, many well-known barges were rebuilt, converted and motorised, including *Hydrogen*, *Phoenician*, *Vicunia*, *Edith May* and *Trilby*. They also built versions of the East Coast barge-yacht, this being a scaled-down model of the real thing with the hold fitted out as accommodation. From the inception of the company, it had been engaged in the construction of auxiliary Naval craft and, with the expansion of this programme due to the war, the adjacent and larger building premises of Wills and Packham Ltd. were acquired. Following the cessation of hostilities, however, and the virtual demise of the Thames barge, such extensive premises were no longer required and the main buildings were turned over to other uses, so that around 1952/53 the former Sittingbourne Shipbuilding Company became a warehousing business.

Shortly after this, the other three comparatively small shipyards, run by Bowater, Burley and A.P.C.M., also closed, because their owners no longer used water-borne transport. So now, apart from the activities of the ballast barge and those of a ship-breaking firm, the Creek has no commercial use. It is, however, still a subject of study for historians and archaeologists, despite the malodorous nature of the severely polluted water and silt.

### Architecture

Sittingbourne and District has never been renowned for the quality or beauty of its buildings. In many guide books Sittingbourne's long High Street is, if described at all, often called 'ordinary' or 'drab'. In fact, the only High Street building which catches the eye is the United Reformed (formerly Congregational) church. When built in the middle of the last century, the church was given a lofty and elegant spire which has proudly overlooked the town ever since. The 13th-century parish church of St Michael's is also sited in the High Street but is not architecturally outstanding; located at the foot of a hill, it is not dominating either. Of the other High Street buildings, the *Bull Inn* (built *c.*1750), with its cream-washed Georgian frontage, is probably the most pleasing, followed by Brenchley House, built in 1779. The High Street would have been more attractive if so many of the older, mostly Georgian, buildings had not been spoilt by the later addition of ugly shop fronts.

Elsewhere in Sittingbourne, Garfield House in Park Road is of particular merit. This was built towards the end of the last century for Daniel Wills, a co-founder and director of the local brickmaking firm of Wills and Packham. The company owned some 30 spritsail barges which regularly sailed in and out of Milton Creek. Daniel had a tall, elegant spire with gabled windows styled into the roof so that he could look out over the other roof-tops and see his barges sailing in the Creek. The building now houses offices.

Also worthy of mention are two wooden buildings beside Milton Creek. These are the sail loft and forge of the former Burley spritsail barge repair yard. The latter is interesting in that the upright timbers are intricately decorated barge tillers – it was built in about 1890 when tillers were being discarded in favour of wheels as a means of steering. The site is now a barge museum.

Probably the best architecture in the area can be found in Milton Regis, where the High Street consists largely of colourful cream-washed and timbered buildings, although many have been spoilt by the addition of unsympathetic shop-fronts. In the centre is the district's pride and joy, the Court Hall, a very attractive and unspoilt example of such buildings. Dating from 1450, the building has been used at various times as a court hall, prison and school. At some point in time, terraced cottages were built on to each end of the hall and, when these became due for demolition in the late 1950s, the Court Hall was threatened as well. Fortunately, however, local interest was such that a fund for saving and restoring the building was started. This was successful and the Court Hall, now detached, with lawns on two sides, makes a most picturesque museum. The display material is aimed mainly at recording the history of the district and its brick, cement, paper and nautical industries. The groups which run the museum are also engaged on the project of restoring the nearby derelict Periwinkle Water Mill and are making good progress. Other buildings in Milton Regis which deserve mention are the parish church of Holy Trinity which has one of the largest towers in England, and the former Congregational church ('Paradise Chapel') whose history was recorded by its minister about a century ago. Unfortunately, this church is no longer used as a place of worship.

At Murston only the two churches are worthy of comment. On the northern outskirts are the disused remains of the original church, Murston Old Church as it is usually called, which dates from *c.*1200. Only one chancel remains – apparently the complete church had three. When Arthur Mee wrote his history of Kent around 1932, the eastern boundary of the churchyard was laid out with flower beds, rockeries and seats, and the grass was always neatly cut; the author described the building as 'a gem of beauty'. In later years the churchyard had long spells as an overgrown wilderness, but in recent times it has been tidied up and the old chancel standing in the middle is very striking. Some of the stones from the old church were used for building the present church, Murston New Church, around 1870. This quite attractive building stands near the centre of Murston.

Sadly, some noteworthy buildings have already disappeared. Sittingbourne's earlier town hall was originally erected as a Corn Exchange in 1859. It stood in the High Street and was of pleasing design, particularly because of its neat clock tower. It became the town hall in 1879 and was demolished in 1961 to make way for Central Avenue, where the same clock can still be seen mounted on a low tower outside the new town hall. To the south of the town was the attractive and unusual mansion known as Gore Court, with its elegant pillars supporting the roof of the front verandah. During the last century it was the home of George Smeed, the famous Sittingbourne industrialist. Later the building became a school, then a hospital during the First World War. It was demolished in 1926 and eventually, in 1937, the beautiful park in which it stood was opened to the public as King George's Playing Field. The bases of the pillars can still be seen there today, and the present pavilion was originally the Gore Court stables. At Milton Regis several attractive old buildings have disappeared, including the *Grapes* public house which was unfortunately demolished to make way for the new roundabout at the bottom of Chalkwell Road.

The district at one time had four castles: Castle Rough, near Kemsley, where the Danes set up camp when they invaded in 893; Bayford Castle, near Milton Creek, where King Alfred gathered troops to resist the Danes; Trim-Tram Castle, north of Murston in the area now called Broome Banks; and Thong Castle, near Bapchild, where the kings of Kent called together their councils in the eighth century. These were very small and there is little evidence of them today except for the moat of Bayford Castle which still exists as a drainage dyke.

**Leisure and Sport**

Artistic societies in Sittingbourne and District are similar to those in other comparable areas; some clubs come and go quickly, others flourish for many years.

The area is well endowed with recreation grounds, all three main settlements having large and level ones so that sports pitches can be laid out with ease. Sittingbourne Recreation Ground is central and also particularly attractive, being lined with tall trees on all sides. It was purchased by the local authority in 1879.

Sittingbourne has always shone in the field of outdoor sport, mainly because the sports clubs have usually been well supported by wealthy local industrialists. Sittingbourne F.C. is of course the biggest local club. For many years this team was held together by the finance and goodwill of local barge-owners and brickmakers; indeed they rescued it from financial disaster and extinction on several occasions. Mr. Jabez Wills (of Wills and Packham) and Messrs. G. Goldsack, F. Hyland and H. Andrews (all of Smeed Dean) were all active club officials at various times.

Formed by a group of amateurs in 1886, from the ashes of the earlier Sittingbourne United F.C., the Club quickly grew in stature and started to field one or two part-time professionals during and after the 1898-99 season. They competed initially in the Kent League, then, after winning the Kent Senior Cup in 1902 and the Kent League in 1903, they competed in the stronger South-Eastern League for several seasons. During this period before the First World War, Sittingbourne, often called 'The Brickies', had many outstanding players. These included the fair-headed halfback Fred 'Snowball' Chandler, who played in the first team for no less than 11 seasons before emigrating to Canada in 1911; and winger Gosnell who played for Sittingbourne for a short time, for Newcastle United (where he won two league championship medals and two F.A. cup runners-up medals), and for England, all in the period 1904-10.

When re-formed after the First World War, the Club had several mediocre seasons before coming back with a resounding bang in 1922. Due to some extensive re-organisation within the Club and deep involvement from the local industrialists, that year marked the start of a glorious part-time professional era. In the next nine seasons, many eminent professional footballers were attracted to the Club by the offer of supporting jobs in local industries. Under the almost continuous captaincy of half-back Bill Dickie, formerly of Chelsea and Stoke City, the Club appeared in the Kent Senior Cup Final no less than five times during that period, winning twice (in 1929 and 1930). The 1929 cup-winning team was, in fact, graced by an international, left-half Plum, who had played previously for Charlton Athletic and England. Sittingbourne was also promoted from the Kent League to the Southern League for three seasons and home gates of 3,000 people at the Bull Ground were quite common.

During this long period of professional football, a local amateur player appeared in the team for a while and later reached great heights. George Watson is worth a mention in this book because he was a member of the family which owned the watermill in Chalkwell Road, just north of the railway line, and also the Milton hoy barges *Constance*, *Hope* and *Orient*. George moved away from the town and played as an amateur for Corinthians, a leading amateur club of the day, and for Charlton Athletic. His crowning achievement came when he was selected for the England amateur team in the early 1930s. George was also a very fine cricketer.

Returning to Sittingbourne F.C., the expense of running such an accomplished team eventually became too much and the departure of Bill Dickie in 1931 coincided with the reversion of the club to mainly amateur players. They did, however, usually field one or two part-time professionals to steady the team, such as the ex-Arsenal, Portsmouth and Ireland full-back Mackie, who appeared for a season or two in the late 1930s. In 1936 the Club celebrated its Golden Jubilee. Bill Dickie, then aged 42 and resident in the town, turned out with his team of old-timers from the Sittingbourne sides of the 1920s, and they achieved a 2-2 draw with the existing Sittingbourne First XI. The game was followed in the evening by a reunion dinner at the *Bull Hotel*.

Since the Second World War, Sittingbourne teams have been mainly amateur, competing in the Kent League. There was, however, a spell of total part-time professionalism for more than a decade from the mid-1950s to the mid-1960s. One 'big-name' player during this era was the ex-Liverpool and Wales goal-keeper Cyril Sidlow, who spent a season or two with 'The Brickies'. Southern League soccer again came to the town for a few years, with the same result as before – financial disaster. There was one player who served for most of this period, half-back Harold Brockington, and he may have equalled or even surpassed the long-service record set by 'Snowball' Chandler half a century before. Also, like 'Snowball', who obtained a Kent Senior Cup winner's medal in 1902, Harold gained this award in 1958 when Sittingbourne won the trophy for the fourth and last time.

With the decline of the local barge, brick and cement industries and the general loss of interest in live football in the south, Sittingbourne F.C. has declined also. The Bull Ground's grandstand and extensive terracing, trimmed in the Club colours of black and red, were put there in the palmy days, but now see only about 130 spectators at a home game. The loss of public interest in live entertainment and activities in the south of England over the last 15 years has indeed been quite startling.

Edward Lloyd Ltd., owners of the local paper mills and also of a fleet of barges, lighters and tugs, used to run a works amateur football team. Lloyd's F.C. ('The Papermakers') were very prominent in Kent League football between about 1930 and 1952 and their greatest success was winning the Kent Amateur Cup in 1950. Like some of Sittingbourne F.C.'s amateurs, a number of Lloyd's players represented Kent over the years and one, Tommy Hopper, who was with them for many seasons, went on further to gain England amateur international honours. Also ex-Football League players were sometimes persuaded to join Lloyd's, though as amateurs, by the offer of good jobs in the paper mills. In fact, some Sittingbourne F.C. players moved to Lloyd's for the same reason. Tommy Hopper was, apparently, the only locally-born footballer to play at international level apart from George Watson. He left Lloyd's in 1947 to join Bromley, with whom he won an F.A. Amateur Cup winner's medal in 1948. He then moved on to Canterbury City and Faversham Town. Tom died at the early age of 56 in 1972; by that time he was resident in Faversham and he was buried in Ospringe churchyard on the outskirts of the town. Lloyd's, later renamed Bowater-Lloyd F.C., declined rapidly in the 1950s and 1960s but their superb ground, now owned by U.K. Paper, gives evidence of their wonderful years in the Kent League.

Several of the cricket clubs in Sittingbourne are very well known, including Bowater-Lloyd and, in particular, Gore Court C.C., who play at the picturesque ground called 'The Grove' which was given to the town by the Smeed-Dean-Andrews partnership. Gore Court also runs ladies' and men's hockey teams, which play at the Grove and, before the First World War, they used to run a football side as well. These Gore Court teams, plus a public house, a road and a Smeed Dean barge, were all named after George Smeed's mansion, Gore Court House. George Smeed was, in fact, the founder of Gore Court C.C. and the teams played initially in the grounds of the mansion.

A new outdoor sport has appeared on the scene in recent years – rugby. Sittingbourne now has a club which plays on the town recreation ground. Indoor sport has also gained in popularity over the last 20 years and Sittingbourne now has facilities for swimming, fitness, martial arts and squash among others.

***

**Postcards, Old Pictures and the Authors**

The first English postcard dates from 1870. This was simply a plain card issued by the Post Office, sold for the price of the halfpenny stamp imprinted on the card, and offered as an alternative to a letter. The private printing and publishing of postcards did not, however, get properly under way until 1894, when legislation was introduced which enabled such cards to be accepted by the Post Office for transmission at the normal rate. The size and type of card in use at this time was both smaller and more formal in appearance than the postcard we know today, and the whole of one side was reserved for the address. Later, with manufacturers pressing for more space for the picture, the card was redesigned, the proportions being altered to conform more nearly to the Continental pattern, and the law was amended to allow the address to be written on the same side as the message. These changes were finally completed in 1902. The front of the card now carried the impression of a picture, print or photograph, and the pictorial effect was often heightened by overprinting in colour. The clarity of reproduction of some of these early cards is remarkable, and many of the best pictures were printed abroad in Saxony and Bavaria. By the end of the Edwardian era, the giving and sending of postcards had become such a feature of daily life that they were being printed by the million, while the subjects ranged from birthdays to battleships, and christenings to cemeteries.

Hidden among all these cards, and awaiting discovery by a future generation, were many fascinating records of everyday scenes in British towns and villages. Yet, sadly for the collector of today, only a small proportion of cards have survived, the vast majority having been lost or destroyed with the passing of time. Postcard collection, or deltiology, is today big business; it has thousands of devotees, and postcard societies in this country and in Germany, France and America are flourishing. In addition, the publication of books and booklets, containing sets of facsimile reproductions of old postcards, has become quite common.

This book, however, goes further. Whilst the authors own considerable numbers of postcards, they also collect photographs, prints and paintings of a historical nature related to the Sittingbourne area. Some of these are the originals, but many more have been painstakingly acquired by borrowing originals and making or obtaining copy negatives and prints. Additionally, much careful research and cross-checking has been done in order to ensure, as far as possible, accuracy in the captions which accompany the selection of their pictures presented below.

The authors are all natives of Sittingbourne. Whilst Alan Cordell now lives in London, he has nevertheless retained his interest in the Swale area. His main studies and activities are related to the history of Milton Creek. However, the majority of pictures are from the collection of Bill and Margaret Lee. They have lived in Sittingbourne all their lives and have made a hobby of collecting pictures and articles of local historical interest. Part of their vast photographic collection has been copied on to transparencies, so Bill and Margaret have become well known in the town for their entertaining and popular historical slide-shows.

Sittingbourne and Milton Regis have changed enormously over the years. This book has been compiled with the aim of giving a good overall appraisal of the appearance of the town, and the lives of its residents, in bygone days.

# The Plates

1. A pageant set out at two o'clock on the afternoon of 18 June 1904 from Snips Hill. Chief Marshal Captain Hedley Peters led the parade on horseback. Bands of the *Daily Chronicle* Paper Mill, Borden Grammar School Cadets and St John's Ambulance Brigade marched in the procession which ended at Prentis Quay with the launching of the lifeboat, in which local dignitaries were taken for a trip. Mrs. Frank Grayling and the ladies of the lifeboat auxiliary carried collecting boxes. The previous year 129 cities and towns had taken part in organised collections for the Royal National Lifeboat Institution which raised thousands of pounds for the fund.

2. The Co-operative Society, with 97 members, opened its tiny two-window shop in East Street in 1874. In 1877 the new premises seen in the centre of this picture were built. The Co-operative Society was a great success and in 1928 new premises were built adjoining the old ones. To celebrate the opening, five per cent discount was given to all customers for seven days. By 1929 there were 7,040 members. To the extreme right can be seen the United Methodist church, which at the present time is being used as a gymnasium. This view dates from *c.*1904.

3. The Co-operative Society branch in Station Street, Sittingbourne, was opened in 1904. This photograph was taken just after the opening.

4. The Co-operative Society's steam bakery at Murston: the opening ceremony on 10 June 1905. This building is now being used as a furniture warehouse.

5. Children of employees of the steam bakery dressed ready for a carnival in 1919.

6. The Co-operative Society of Sittingbourne held a demonstration every year. In the early years they were held a Murston Rectory Park, later Albany Meadows was used and then Cryalls Lane. Tea was given to all children unde 14 years and widows who were members, as well as old people and children from the Milton Union. Children in thi procession can be seen carrying their own mugs. At one Co-operative demonstration over 12,000 people assemblec in three separate fields.

HOUSE
HUBBARD

7. Milton Regis town hall as it looked in about 1900, with the local fire brigade, possibly celebrating the arrival of a new fire appliance. The town hall was demolished in 1938.

8. Crescent Street fire station was opened in 1897. Milton Regis and Sittingbourne fire brigades amalgamated in 1930 when this new steamer was bought to replace the old one which had been acquired by public subscription in 1900. Driver Brooker drove the new engine from Dennis of Guildford to Sittingbourne on 5 April 1930.

9. This impressive scene photographed in 1903 shows the Sittingbourne fire brigade parading through the High Street. They entered the Steam Drill Competitions and several times won the championship, being considered the finest brigade in the county.

10. Sittingbourne and Milton Regis fire brigades combined to fight the fire at Sheppey Glue Works on 30 May 1920. The fire was in the department where the sulphuric acid was kept. The containers of acid were leaking and fumes made the work very hazardous. The glue department was untouched, so work resumed as normal the following day.

11. Milton Regis fire brigade was established on 14 February 1884 at Crown Road. The Chief Officer then was Mr. Watson of *The Coniston*, London Road. In 1928 the premises were renovated and extended by Messrs. Bowes Bros. In the centre of this photograph is Councillor Mr. Perce Jeffreys, opening the new fire station. A new engine had been purchased 12 months earlier but was found to be too large for the old premises. Mrs. Maundrell J.P. poured a glass of champagne over the bonnet of the new engine and named her *Mary*.

12. The manual fire pump shown here was used for nearly 60 years by Milton Regis fire brigade. It was renovated by F. Littlewood & Sons in 1939 and stored at the parish church, Milton Regis. Years later Bowater's fire brigade collected the pump from a shed at the vicarage and restored it to working order. The fire pump was built in 1829 and is now preserved in a museum. The men are, left to right, Mr. John Waters, Mr. Reg Fletcher and Mr. Mick Stone.

13. The 2nd Milton Regis Scout Troop in 1920. They always held their meetings in the parish rooms at St Paul's Street. The Scout Master sitting centre right was Mr. Horace Greensted and his assistant on his right was Mr. Stanley Tong.

14. Crowds of people gathered in Milton Regis on 28 November 1906 to watch a procession marching to Holy Trinity parish church to unveil a memorial to two local men who were killed in the South African war: Major George Ray of the 5th Northumberland Fusiliers, who fell at Magersfontein; and Sergeant Albert Willson of the 7th Dragoon Guards, who fell at Sand River.

15. Post card of Milton Regis High Street early this century. To the extreme left can be seen part of Mr. Strouts' butcher's shop, next to C. Pillow's ironmongery. Centre left is Mr. Edmund Pillow's drapery.

16. This area of Milton Regis High Street has completely changed today. The shop on the left was Reynolds' and later became Tames', where most local residents bought their shoes. The chemist's shop (right front) was owned by Mr. Maundrell and later by Mr. Boar. At every really high tide this whole area flooded. Today Tannery Court, a residential home for the elderly, stands on this site.

17. Milton Regis High Street looking towards Milton Hill. Hinde House can be seen centre left next to a fruit and baker's shop and a post office where Mr. Knowles was sub-postmaster. Later, the post office moved across the street to its present location.

18. The Court Hall of Milton Regis was built in 1450. It was a meeting place for the court with two prison cells below. At other times it was used as a school. This photograph, *c.*1935, shows the Court Hall when it adjoined a row of houses. In 1958 the building was restored and is now used as a museum run jointly by the Sittingbourne Archaeology Group and the Sittingbourne Society.

19. Milton Regis High Street as it looked in 1912. The old town hall (which had originally been a market) opened in 1803, was demolished in 1938, and was replaced in 1939 by the public library. The horse and van on the left belonged to Moses Goldsmith, a baker and confectioner from Berry Street. Milton Regis has a history that dates back to Saxon times. Most of the houses are 18th-century and earlier. The original Market House stood in the middle of the street near the junction of Crown Road and High Street. The clock bell was cast at Borden in 1631.

20. This photograph, *c.*1913, shows Mr. Thomas Clark's shop at 8 Chalkwell Road, Milton Regis, next to the *Grapes* public house. Outside the shop can be seen Jane Ellen Clark with her son Arthur and daughter Elsie. It remained a shop until the late 1940s and was demolished in 1957; a roundabout stands on this site today.

21. Joseph Simmons' shop was situated at 17 Church Street, Milton Regis. This photograph was taken just after the turn of the century and probably shows Mr. Simmons standing proudly in the doorway of his shop with his son. The shop has since been demolished and new houses have now been built nearby.

22. Troops in Milton Regis High Street during the 1914-18 War; possibly cadets in training, having a rest after a day's marching. Many troops were billeted in this area during the Great War.

23. A memorial to the old boys of Milton Regis Council Schools who were killed in the 1914-18 War. The two scouts standing either side are Cyril Tong and Ernest Green.

24. On Friday 1 October 1920, all the widows and children of the men of Milton Regis killed in the 1914-18 War assembled at Ufton Lane Council School where tea and entertainments were arranged. All the children were given socks or stockings, cakes and sweets, and were presented with a mug made by the W. H. Goss company. This is one of the mugs, decorated with the Milton Regis coat of arms.

25. Hibbins' shop in Flushing Street, photographed just before it was pulled down. This area of Milton Regis was completely demolished in the late 1940s and 1950s.

26. No. 1 Bridge Street, Milton Regis, which was not far from the busy Creek and was used early this century as a Salvation Army Hall. This part of Milton Regis was demolished in the 1950s.

27. Rock Road, Milton Regis, showing the shop and sub-post office on the corner, which at this time (*c.*1908) was owned by Mr. Marshall.

28. Milton Regis Bowling Club was founded in 1540 and is the second oldest club in this country. Milton Regis Butts had been an archery site before the bowling green was laid. In 1939 it was changed from a crown green to an association green.

29. This photograph was taken of Bowling Club members over 60 years ago.

30. A walking race in West Street, Sittingbourne. The public house seen centre is the *Golden Fleece*, still standing today. The railings on the right belong to the *Volunteers Inn* which has since been demolished. This photograph was taken, *c.*1902, by Mr. Pavey, a builder with premises in West Street, who was a keen amateur photographer.

31. In June 1902 crowds gathered to welcome home the Exactive Service Squad returning from fighting in the South African War, in which 22,000 officers and men had lost their lives. The photograph by Mr. Pavey shows Timothy White's (extreme left) next to Railway Terrace.

32. A lovely photograph taken by Mr. Pavey of a church outing to Woodstock Park, *c.*1902. Mr. John Andrews, a well-known Murston man who became a director of Smeed Dean Ltd., is sitting in the centre of the second row from the back, and Mr. William Roper, Headmaster of the Wesleyan School, East Street, is on the left at the front.

33. Probably a darts team outing photographed in 1912 outside the *Royal Oak*, Dover Street, now known as the *British Legion*. The landlord was Mr. Horace Neaves, seen standing fifth from left behind his son.

34. A postcard of Chalkwell showing the *King's Head*. On the corner of Borden Lane stood the *King William IV* which has since been demolished. To the right of the *King's Head* stood a horse trough which has now been re-erected in Johnson House Gardens to hold plants.

35. An outing from the *Lion Inn* which stood at the corner of Mill Street, Milton Regis. This public house, once surrounded by houses which have now been demolished, has been converted to a private dwelling. This photograph was taken in about 1920.

36. This photograph shows the *Green Dragon* public house which stood in King Street, Milton Regis. The landlord in this picture, taken about 1920, was Mr. George Cockell, seen here with Mr. Arthur Lewis and his niece Daisy. Both public house and street were demolished about 1955.

37. This postcard shows the *Coniston Hotel* as it looked earlier this century. It has since been greatly altered and enlarged.

38. The *Alexandra Hotel*, formerly spelt Alexander, at the corner of Church Street and Charlotte Street. Bowater's Mill (now U.K. Paper) can be seen in the background. The hotel was demolished in about 1960.

39. The *Billet* public house, London Road, showing the landlord Mr. Thomas Moor holding his granddaughter in his arms, about 1906. The new *Billet* public house was built in 1928 and now stands back from the road, a completely detached building.

40. A view of Key Street, *c.*1917. Looking towards Keycol Hill on the left is the Primitive Methodist chapel, now demolished; on the right is one of the entrances to the Grove.

41. Good accommodation at 6d. a night for cyclists was offered by the landlord of the *Key Inn*. In 1896 the *Key Inn*, with good stabling, yards, garden and meadow land, was let at a rent of £46 per annum. These buildings have now made way for a very busy roundabout.

42. Formerly Nos. 1 & 2 Old Cottages, Chestnut Street. This is a timber-framed 16th-century Grade II listed building. A new road has now been built which bypasses the street.

43. A water cart laying the dust at Holly Bank Hill, *c.*1914. This area, which was almost completely residential a few years ago, is now becoming more commercial.

44. A view of West Street looking toward the High Street, *c.*1907. On the right can be seen the horse and van of Cremer & Sons outside their premises next to the Roman Catholic church. The house, centre left, on the corner of Hawthorn Road, was demolished and a garage now stands on the site.

45. Mr. Tom Reynolds with W. J. Cremer & Sons' horse and van. This photograph was taken in the Gore Court Road area.

46. A traffic jam opposite Crescent Street in Sittingbourne High Street, *c.*1907. On the left are the large premises of Croft's the pawnbrokers next to Dan Easton's china and earthenware shop.

47. Dan Easton's china and earthenware shop at No. 92 High Street, *c.*1914. At the corner of Crescent Street, Edward Marsh had a draper's shop and opposite were the premises of Mr. Bloxham, a hairdresser and wig maker.

48. A postcard of West Street, *c.*1914, looking towards Holly Bank Hill. In the background on the right can be seen the Ebenezer Gospel Hall which was erected in 1903 and later became the Salvation Army meeting place. The garage on the left belonged to Cleaver & Co.

49. The post office was opened by Mrs. G. H. Dean of Whitehall, Bell Road, Sittingbourne, in 1912. It was demolished about 1961 when the new post office opened in Central Avenue. This view dates from *c.*1917.

50. A view of the High Street with the Baptist Tabernacle on the right. The future of this building is at present under discussion. On the opposite corner, the chemist's shop belonged to John French – it was also an optician's and a sub-post office.

51. A postcard, *c.*1917, showing the premises of Albert Webb & Son, a fishmonger of 71 High Steet, Sittingbourne, who also had a shop at 60 West Street. On the extreme left is Martin's Bank.

52. A view of the High Street with the *Bull Hotel*, a coaching inn for more than 600 years, licensed by the monks of Chilham Castle in the 12th century. The present building, dating from *c.*1750, was renovated and modernised in the early 1970s. On the right, Woolworth's and several adjoining shops now stand on the site of the *Rose Inn*, built in 1708 – a superb hotel where Princess Victoria and her mother, the Duchess of Kent, stayed in 1825.

53. The photographer has climbed St Michael's church tower to secure this aerial view along Sittingbourne High Street, *c.*1895.

54. Sittingbourne High Street, looking west, *c.*1895.

55. This photograph taken in 1903 shows, extreme right, the *Three Post Boys Inn*, an early 19th-century building next to Taylor & Son, jeweller and silversmith. On the extreme left is the International Tea Company Stores.

56. A view of Sittingbourne High Street with the double kerb outside Mr. Grant's premises. Mr. Grant was surveyor to the Sittingbourne Urban District Council. On the left can be seen the gates of the Wesleyan church.

57. The Wesleyan church after bomb damage during the Second World War. The church has since been rebuilt.

58. This postcard shows the premises of John Whibley, gentlemen's outfitter, next to the path leading to the Butts and Railway Station. Opposite is the entrance to the brewery which later became the Queen's Laundry and then the Queen's Cinema in 1912.

59. To the right of this view of Sittingbourne High Street can be seen Mr. Sidney Boulding's butcher's shop called Church House, which in the late 1930s was one of the buildings which made way for the Odeon Cinema. On the left, Alfred Reynolds had his furnishing premises next to Hulburds & Son. This photograph was taken *c.*1910.

60. The Bell Road junction with the High Street. A cinema now stands on the site of the London Bazaar. Ambrose's grocer's shop is on the opposite side, next to Fremlin's, brewers and wine and spirit merchants.

61. This postcard, *c.*1917, shows the *Three Kings Hotel* which stood on the corner of Bell Road and East Street. Mr. Walter Tucker the landlord certainly believed in advertising! There is one solitary horse and a cyclist in the street.

62. A view of East Street looking towards St Michael's church, *c.*1906. On the left where the cart stands is George Barry's blacksmith's shop with Shipp Newsagency next door. On the opposite side, extreme right, the Maidstone and District bus office now stands.

63. The Co-operative Society occupied premises on both sides of East Street, consisting of 10 different departments. There is no road to South Avenue in this photograph, taken *c.*1904, as it was not built until 1930.

64. West Street in the 1920s. The shops on the right stood on the corner of Dover Street and have long since disappeared.

65. The High Street *c.*1937. The old post office is on the right and in the middle distance is the distinctive clock tower of the old town hall, built as a corn exchange in the middle of the last century. Both buildings have been demolished. The elegant spire of the Congregational church is visible in the background.

66. The east end of the High Street, *c.*1937. The motor car has certainly ousted the horse and cart by this time.

67. In July 1921 a royal visit was made to Milton Regis, Sittingbourne, Murston and Teynham by His Royal Highness the Duke of York, who later became King George VI. He is seen here inspecting a Guard of Honour at Lloyd's Mill, Sittingbourne, consisting of 333 ex-servicemen. Also, long-service awards were presented to some of the employees.

68. This photograph, taken outside the *Peace and Plenty* public house in Milton Road, shows His Royal Highness meeting local dignitaries, with the fire brigade standing in the background.

69. The next stop for the royal party was a visit to Burley's brickfields where the Duke can be seen presenting an award to Mr. William Mills of Charlotte Street. Three of the Burley brothers appear in the photograph.

70. Another photograph of the Duke in one of Burley's brickfields with some members of the Burley family.

71. The Duke with his arms full of apples, chatting and laughing with the people in Mr. Dean's orchard at Bell Road.

72. The Duke was entertained for lunch by Mr. and Mrs. Dean at Whitehall, Bell Road. Sitting next to the Duke is Mrs. Dean; standing left to right are Mrs. Tylden, the Marchioness of Queensbury, Colonel Locke, Mr. Dean, the Marquess of Camden, Sir Bertram Boyce, Mr. W. G. Bones, Mr. Frank Lloyd, Lord and Lady Harris and Mr. Ketchem.

73. The thatched shelter in Sittingbourne Recreation Ground about 1905. It stood opposite the end of Connaught Road and was demolished in about 1960.

74. The tree-lined passage on the east side of Sittingbourne Recreation Ground in 1905. It still looks similar today.

75. A view of the Grove, Key Street, *c.*1909. The inhabitants of Sittingbourne and Milton have Mr. George Andrews to thank for the gift of Grove Park which he offered to the people for their pleasure and recreation. A memorial tablet was unveiled in the park in July 1937.

76. A cricket match at Woodstock Park early this century. Pistock is the ancient name for Woodstock Park, a manor which at one time belonged to a Benedictine Monastery at Minster, Sheppey. The house was built by Sir Abraham Chambers in about 1780; more recently it was owned by the Earl of Westmorland, and then a Captain Gilliat. In June 1945 Woodstock Farm and 250 acres of land were sold at an auction in the *Bull* yard for £24,000. It then became a Shell Research establishment as it is today.

77. A great hospital fête was held at King George's Park on 25 July 1939. The fête was opened by the Lord Mayor of London, seen here with his wife and Captain Hedley Peters, Chief Officer of the Fire Brigade. Earlier they had visited the Memorial Hospital which had been donated to the town by Mrs. Garwood in memory of her parents, Mr. and Mrs. Frank Lloyd. A physical training exhibition, boxing tournaments and other entertainments took place and the fête ended with dancing. Every 6d. given for an official programme was donated to hospital funds.

78. Gore Court, an ancient manor, was owned and rebuilt by Mr. Gabriel Harper in 1791. Mr. George Smeed later bought it and lived there until his death in 1881. A Mr. de Winton turned it into a boys' boarding school for a time and during the Great War it was used as a hospital by the Royal Army Medical Corps. The only remaining parts of the house are the stables (which were turned into the sports pavilion) and the bases of the frontal pillars. On Saturday 2 October 1937 a fête was held at Gore Court Park, opened by Lord Harris of Belmont, when its name was changed to King George's Field.

79. Probably a draft of the Queen's Regiment marching off to France, seen here in Park Road on their way to the railway station. To the right of the men would have been the *Gore Court Arms* public house, still standing today.

80. A photograph of a company of the Sussex Regiment marching in West Street, Sittingbourne, *c.*1914. On the right of the street can be seen Hogben's newsagency and tobacconist's shop next to Edward Foster's greengrocery. On the left stood the old *Volunteers Inn*, now demolished.

81. A photograph of Unity Street taken in July 1916 after it was hit in a Zeppelin raid, showing the damage caused to people's homes.

82. A photograph of Mill Street looking towards Lloyd's Mill, showing its famous cobbled street. The public house on the left was the *Waterman's Arms*. Thomas Buggs, a well-known local councillor, had his grocer's shop on the opposite side. This street and surrounding area were demolished around 1955.

83. Papermaking has been a major industry at Sittingbourne since the middle of the last century. This is Lloyd's Mill in about 1925, showing the prominent chimney shaft which has since been demolished.

84. An overhead view of Sittingbourne from the top of Lloyd's Paper Mill shaft, taken about 1895. The shaft's shadow can be seen in the foreground.

85. A view from Lloyd's shaft, showing Milton, *c.*1895. The elegant house in the foreground was occupied by the Paper Mill manager and was later demolished when the Mill was extended. Beyond, the spars and furled sails of a barge at Milton Creek Head can be seen and Milton church is just visible in the background.

86. On 5 January 1907 Lloyd's Paper Mill at Sittingbourne had its second great fire in seven years. It was attended by nine brigades which consisted of 120 firemen. The shed which housed number 11 paper-making machine, considered to be the finest in the world, was destroyed.

87. The boilerhouse the day after the fire. Mr. Frank Lloyd would not let the men be stood off – everyone was encouraged to help clear up and get the rebuilding started as soon as possible.

88. This picture of Lloyd's Mill, *c.*1916, shows clearly the pond which supplied the water and was later filled in when a water tower was erected.

89. In 1923, Lloyd opened Kemsley Paper Mill on a site some two miles north of Sittingbourne. This photograph shows the mill in its original state; it has since been greatly extended. This mill, like the one at Sittingbourne, was taken over by Bowater in the 1930s; both recently passed to U.K. Paper.

90. The laying of the foundation stone at Kemsley Mill; Mr. Frank Lloyd can be seen standing in the centre with other local dignitaries. The mill was opened in 1923.

91. Kemsley Village, which Lloyd built to house the mill workers, as it looked about 1925. It has a similar appearance today.

92. A photograph of the ladies working at Lloyd's Wharf during the 1914-18 War.

93. This photograph was taken inside Bowater's Sittingbourne Mill during 1945. The workers were producing compressed cardboard shell cases and jettison fuel tanks. The ladies were given extra rations of milk because of the chemicals used in the process of making the tanks. They worked a shift system with a day work gang as well. Reg Bush, seated centre, was in charge.

94. This photograph, captioned 'Carpave, Bell Road, Sittingbourne', shows the Memorial Hospital which was given to the town by the family of Mr. Frank Lloyd as a memorial to him. He died shortly before it was completed. Carpave was a new type of road surfacing being used. The photograph was taken around 1930.

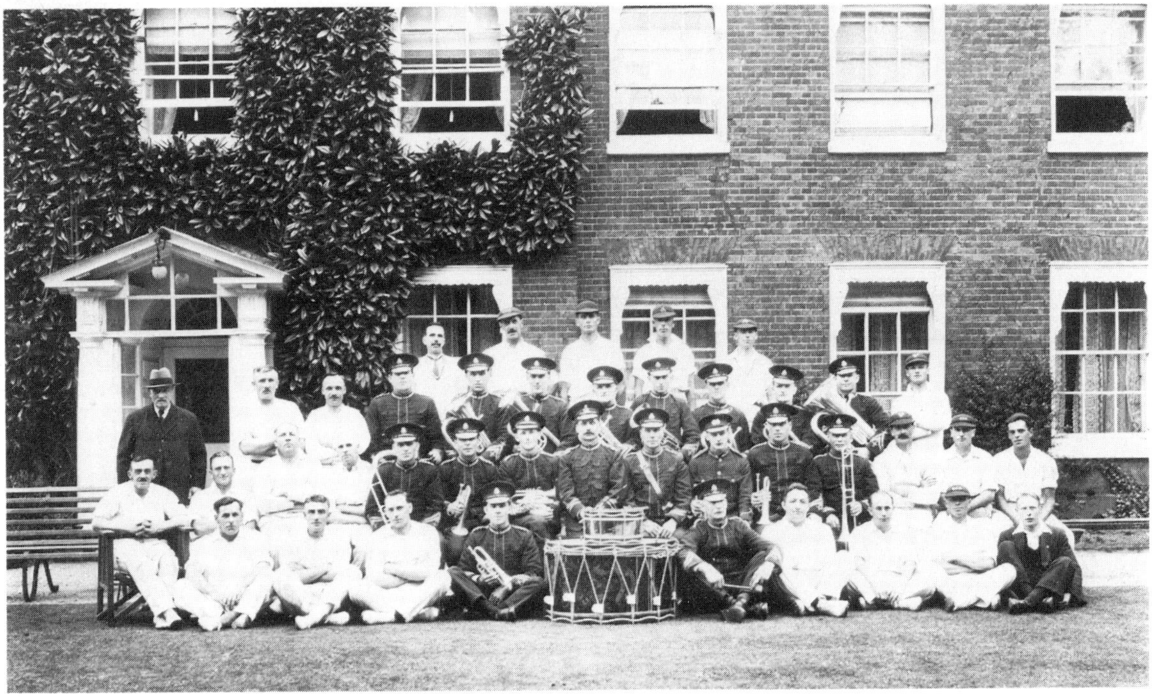

95. As a further memorial to Mr. Frank Lloyd, who died in 1927, visits were arranged each year for the Lloyd's band and cricket team to travel to Coombe Park, Shirley, near Croydon. Motor buses would pick up the players and pensioners at Dover Street, Sittingbourne. Colonel Garwood, standing extreme left, who was Mr. Lloyd's son-in-law, would arrange a match with the local cricket team. This photograph dates from about 1929.

96. *Daily Chronicle* football team, 1898-99 season. This team was later renamed Lloyd's. Top row, left to right: H. Jacob (Trainer), P. Hickman (Linesman), H. J. Summers (Referee), W. Gammon, J. Williams, W. J. Douse, G. Gooden. Middle row, left to right: A. Cole, E. Mungham, H. Rouse, A. Vandepeer, J. Moore, M. Jeffery. Front row, left to right: W. Jones, E. Williams, J. Steers, T. Hadler.

97. Lloyd's reserves, who won the Kent Junior Cup in the 1936-37 season. Top row, left to right: G. Whitbread, A. Ottaway, R. Cockell, A. S. Wood, F. J. Brenchley, W. Hammond, C. Mellor, A. R. Watson, L. J. Goldfinch, H. Hills, Mr. W. Jones (Trainer). Bottom row, left to right: Mr. F. Leeds, Mr. W. Hilliard, J. A. Drake, H. Wills, G. B. Thorogood, A. J. Fryday, Mr. R. B. Miller.

98. Milton Athletic, 1931-32 season. Back row, left to right: Bill Smith, Fred Taylor, Arthur Bartlett, Ted Morris, Mick Stone, Harry Smith, Arthur Hawkes and Ernest Mann. Middle row, left to right: Alf Hills, Frank Catt, Fred Mount, Jack Hobbs, Albert Wyles, Jim Bugden and Jumbo Kemp. Front row, left to right: Wally Lumby, Nobby Holdstock, Marshall Brunger. Wally Lumby later played in the Kent League with Lloyd's and Sittingbourne, also in the Football League (First Division) with Grimsby Town.

99. A charity football match between the Post Office and the Railway in 1912. Seated in the centre is Colonel Lumley Webb of Tunstall, with nurse Jenkins on his left.

100. Street parties were held all over the country to celebrate the Coronation of King George VI and Queen Elizabeth ir 1937. This party in Pembury Street is enjoying a sing-along accompanied by two accordions. Councillor Mr. Bedelle stands in the centre. The Pembury Street houses have now been demolished and a residential home for the elderly built o the site.

101. This party was held in Charlotte Street. The children are all seated enjoying their tea. Later there was dancing in the street.

102. Kingsmill Road was the venue for this Coronation street party. Mr. Len Baker (Chairman of the Sittingbourne and Milton Urban District Council) and Mr. Tom Buggs and his wife (who had a grocery just round the corner in Mill Street) can be seen in the crowd. Kingsmill Road has now been demolished and a dairy stands on the site.

103. Working on the farm was essential for the housewife struggling to feed her family. Here we see Mrs. Amy Wigg, a well-known local lady, standing on the ladder in the centre with her son Jack sitting centre front, picking fruit with friends and neighbours in about 1920.

104. A lovely photograph taken about 1904 of some local ladies in the hop gardens. Judging by their appearance, they probably knew they were to have their photograph taken and dressed up for the occasion.

105. The Wesleyan School, East Street, was built in 1834 and enlarged in 1873 to accommodate 296 children. The Headmaster was Mr. William Henry Roper. This school was closed when the new Council School opened on 27 June 1910. The Wesleyan School made way for the Empire Theatre, later the Plaza Cinema; this latter building was also eventually demolished. It is a great pity that such a splendid picture is now cracked.

106. A class of boys at the new Council School, 1911.

107. A later photograph of Sittingbourne Council School taken in 1922. Mr. Heaps, the Headmaster, is standing on the right and Mr. Mobbs on the left.

108. St Paul's Infant School was erected in Kingsmill Road, Milton Regis in 1870 for 71 children. This photograph was taken in 1908 just before the school was due to close.

109. Milk was first delivered to schools in about 1930. In this photograph the children of Ufton Lane School are happily drinking their milk, which cost a halfpenny. The teacher was Miss Stapleton.

110. Milton Regis Butts Boy's School was built in 1898 to accommodate 440 boys. This photograph was taken in 1903 when the Headmaster was Mr. McIsaac.

111. Empire Day at Milton Regis Butts School, *c.*1920. Families of the school children looked forward each year to this occasion. The children saluted the flag and sang the National Anthem. Medals and bars were given to the children for good attendance. Boy Scouts and the Rifle Company of the school marched and drilled before the spectators. The Headmaster Mr. Leeson is seen here conducting the children's singing.

112. Milton Regis Butts Girls' School was erected in 1848 on the site of an earlier small church school and accommodated 474 girls. This photograph was taken in 1920.

113. The County Girls' School, *c.*1909. Brenchley House was built by Edward Brenchley in about 1800. It was used as a Girls' Grammar School for 50 years.

114. The old Borden Grammar School was built in 1878 in the Tudor Gothic style. It was later used by the Kent Farm Institute and is now a college for further education.

115. New Borden Grammar School, *c.*1930, when it was approximately two years old, as was the main grandstand of Sittingbourne Football Club which can be seen beyond the school. Adjacent to the back of the grandstand is the area which formed the cattle market.

116. Milton Regis parish church in about 1905, showing the large lake which used to be nearby. The church was founded in the seventh century and is one of the oldest in Kent. It was practically destroyed by Norse invaders in 1052 and rebuilt in 1070 with an unusually large western tower.

117. The parish church of St Michael photographed early this century. Built of flint and stone in an early English style, it was badly damaged by fire in 1762 and was restored in 1873.

118. Sittingbourne cemetery, *c.*1895, with the elegant chapel/mortuary in the centre. At that time it was considered one of the most beautiful cemeteries in Kent.

119. The waterworks at Highsted opened on Wednesday 7 March 1904. Mr. F. Littlewood, Chairman of Milton Regis Urban Council, was master of ceremonies. Engineer Mr. G. F. Deacon gave a brief talk on how the waterworks was operated with steam and gas engines. The cost of raising 1,000 gallons of water was just 1s. 7d.

120. Sittingbourne Public Baths and Gymnasium at the Butts, Sittingbourne, was built in 1896. The Workmen's Club and Institute was previously the Latimer Congregational chapel. The Butts were targets comprised of earthen mounds for archery practice.

121. St Michael's Mission Room School, previously a church hall, was built to take 160 persons. It was later demolished and a garage forecourt has stood on the site for some years.

122. T. Standen & Sons of 181 Shortlands Road started their new bus service in December 1913, offering penny and halfpenny stages. The through fare from Greenstreet to Rainham was 8d., children half-price if they were over three and under 12 years old. Standen's Depot was at Crescent Street next to the fire station.

123. This photograph was taken in the same year of an outing for Burley's brickfields workers. Travelling for the first time on an open-top omnibus must have been quite an experience.

124. T. Standen & Sons also did continental removals. Right in the background can be seen Wickham House of London Road. This house was taken down and rebuilt at Tunstall. The photograph dates from about 1905.

125. This photograph of May and Sayers of 78 High Street, Sittingbourne, was taken about 1912. Earlier, the shop had been situated on the corner of Berry Street. This was where mothers bought their children's school clothes.

126. Harold Nursery was previously owned by Mr. Monk the builder. Mr. Poggensee was employed by Mr. Monk and then took the business over. He was instructor for the County Council School Gardens. He is seen here with his employees, having won a championship in 1906. Later the nursery was sold to Mr. Castle. A greengrocer's shop and houses now stand on the site.

127. Mr. William Forster, an undertaker of 14 New Road, photographed in 1912 with his twin daughters.

128. The houses of New Road and the Wall as seen in this photograph were completely demolished in the early 1960s. In the background is Bowater's Wharf.

129. Thomas Monk did his apprenticeship with Chrisfield of Milton Regis. He established his own business in 1872. He is seen here laying the drains in Charlotte Street in 1906, which had caused a great deal of trouble due to constant flooding.

130. A photograph taken early this century of road works in West Street, Sittingbourne. The *Volunteers* public house railings can be seen on the right; opposite is Webb's fishmongery, Hogben's newsagency, and Foster's greengrocery.

131. No. 1 Bell Road, the premises of Henry Tidy, builder. Sainsbury's car park now occupies this spot.

132. Packers Bros. basket works at 12 Bell Road, Sittingbourne, a family business, where all kinds of baskets were made. This shop, now demolished, has been replaced by part of Sainsbury's car park.

133. The first motor mail service between Green Street and Sittingbourne. Mr. Charles Hadlow is driving a Douglas motor cycle, equipped with a lovely basket carrier.

134. Employees of James Keiller & Son about 1926. Their business premises were at the corner of London Road and Cryalls Lane, and later became Bugge's insecticide factory.

135. A carnival float photographed in 1918, just after the end of the war. The caption on the float reads, 'We have lost our ration cards but we're still smiling'. The ladies all probably worked at Lloyd's Wharf. In the background is Sittingbourne railway station.

136. In 1927 these ladies who worked at the Queen's Laundry played a football match against the ladies who worked at the jam factory. Unfortunately no photograph of the other team seems to have survived and the score is not known.

137. A photograph taken early this century, showing Senior's Sanitary Laundry cart with plenty of advertising telling of moderate prices for the family's washing. This shop was at 96 High Street, Milton Regis, next to the Cross.

138. Bill Boakes holding the horse's bridle with his brother Len sitting on the cart in Faith Street, Sittingbourne. There were nine houses in Faith Street all of which have now been demolished. The Swale Borough Council Maintenance Depot stands on the site.

139. Mr. R. A. Hadaway, Chairman of the Sittingbourne Council, at the entrance of the town hall for the arrival of the first motorised cream-coloured ambulance. It was presented to Sittingbourne by Mr. and Mrs. G. H. Dean of Whitehall, Bell Road, in February 1913. Mr. W. Pullen of Park Road Garage had driven the ambulance from Tunbridge Wells to Sittingbourne. Mr. and Mrs. Dean, the latter with a bouquet of flowers, are among the crowds in Sittingbourne High Street. Members of Sittingbourne Fire Brigade, Troop of Boy Scouts and Borden Boy Scouts form a guard of honour.

140. Early this century there were two markets held regularly in Sittingbourne. The corn market was held every Friday at the Town Hall. The cattle market was held fortnightly on Mondays near the *Bull Hotel* meadow, conducted by Mr. F. A. Bensted. Later the cattle market was held every week.

141. Meads Mill at Vicarage Road, Milton Regis, photographed about 1906. At this time the watermill belonged to John Bates, a miller who had a shop in Milton Regis High Street. Mr. Willson, who had a dairy, lived in the mill house. In February 1929, Meads Mill with 10 perches of land was bought by the local council for £135 for use as a recreation ground. The mill pond dried up many years ago and only a small part of the original building is left standing today.

142. The windmill at the Meads, a black smock mill with white cap, also owned by John Bates at this time. Shown on a map dated 1819, it was rebuilt in 1879 by Frank Littlewood. In 1889 an auxiliary steam engine from Chalkwell Mill was installed by Gardiners of Frederick Street. It was not a flour mill but was used for animal feed and bean splitting.

143. The Meads at Milton Regis with the dykes full of water as they used to be many years ago. This photograph, taken early this century, shows the windmill in the background. Unfortunately it has since been demolished.

144. The water for Kingsmill came across Church Street, almost lapping the walls of St Paul's church, on the left in this photograph. The mill pond was fed by a small stream known to local people as the Periwinkle. This area has now completely changed.

145. This photograph was taken in 1905 of the new Kingsferry Bridge, replacing the old bridge which had opened in 1860. Mr. James Spree, standing on the bridge, was awarded a certificate for his work as the engine driver. Kingsferry Bridge was a toll bridge until 1 July 1929. Farmers crossing the bridge with livestock had to pay so much per head. During the 1914-18 War a permit book with photograph was issued to all users of the bridge. A payment of one shilling was charged to replace a lost book.

146. A picturesque view of Tong Mill. For years local people spent a lot of their leisure time here boating, picnicking and feeding the swans and ducks. In the past, baptisms have taken place in Tong Mill stream with water from Thomas à Becket's spring.

147. Tong Mill in 1908, with Mr. Hughes, the mill manager who lived in the mill house, standing in the front. Tong Mill was owned by Mr. Wicks, a miller and baker.

148. Mr. James Terry, blacksmith and wheelwright, whose business premises were situated at Bapchild. This photograph was taken about 1920. A garage now occupies the site.

149. This photograph of local bargemen was taken at Crown Quay Lane in 1921. The newly-built hut to the rear was used for concerts and meetings; the photograph was taken on the opening day.

150. After the opening ceremony of the Bargemen's Hut, there was a procession to Bowes Park led by Mr. Toms of the Salvation Army who was also a bargeman. At the park, entertainment was arranged by the bargemen for families and friends. Mr. Toms is seen in black top hat at the front, leading the people along Crown Quay Lane.

151. Jimmy Toms of Goodnestone Road, with his wife and family in about 1920. They were all devout Salvationists, and the grave in which Jimmy and some of his family are buried in Sittingbourne cemetery has the Salvation Army coat of arms carved on the stonework.

152. The Bargemen's Brotherhood was a social and spiritual organisation for bargemen founded by the Rev. Parry Evans (vicar of St Michael's) before the First World War. The headquarters was the above-mentioned Bargemen's Hut, opposite the *White Hart* in Crown Quay Lane which stood for the period 1921-41. Membership of the Brotherhood entitled one to wear an anchor watch-chain emblem and, when afloat, to fly a 'BB' pennant. This photograph, taken about 1922, shows members of the Brotherhood and their wives gathered for a charabanc outing. In the front row, the Rev. Parry Evans can be seen third from the right. The other gentlemen in the front row are, from left to right, skippers Ted 'Talking Tommy' Wraight (with babes in pram), Henry Attwater, Sid Court, Mannering or Mortley, and Tommy Pearce. In the middle of the group on the coach is skipper George 'Doggy' Fletcher.

153. Brickmaking was a big local industry. This photograph shows one of Burley's brickfields in about 1920.

154. Another local industry was cement manufacture. Of the several factories which have been in commission since about 1850, the one operated by Smeed Dean at Murston was the largest. This is the Smeed Dean works, with a barquentine alongside, in about 1920.

155. Lushington Cottages and Murston School, *c.*1920. The cottages were demolished to make way for two blocks of terraced houses in about 1930.

156. The barge *Yieldsted* at Gransden's Wharf around 1905. Behind her mast are Wills and Packham's barge-building sheds. A little further to the left is a barge lying at Crown Quay, and the warehouse at Filmer's Dock.

157. A view of Milton Parish Wharf around 1905, with the barge *Constance* alongside. She was one of three barges owned by Watson, who also owned the watermill between Chalkwell Road and Charlotte Street. In the background is Prentis Quay, upon which stood the Portreeve's house and the offices of Eastwood & Co., a local brickmaking and barge-owning firm.

158. Lloyd's Wharf, *c.*1905. The cranes stood until about 1968. The barge alongside is the *Pioneer*, which had been built for Lloyd at Conyer in 1898. Note the numerous brickfield chimneys in the background.

159. A busy scene looking down Crown Quay Reach, *c.*1905. The sail loft and forge of Burley's barge yard, both of which stand today, can be seen towards the right of the picture.

160. View from Crown Quay, looking down Bullivant's reach, *c.*1905. The markings in the sprit of the barge in the centre show that she was one of Wills and Packham's. On the right are the barge-building shed and Dolphin Cement Works operated by Burley. The first cement works on this site was Bullivant's Works, established about 1860; it gave its name to this particular reach of Milton Creek.

161. A picture which epitomises the bustling activity in Milton Creek earlier this century. This is Adelaide Dock in 1930, with seven Smeed Dean barges at the wharves. The nearest barge is the *Histed*, next to her is the *Argosy*, and second from the right with the short topmast is the *Leslie*.

162. Loading bricks into the barge *Histed* at Adelaide Dock in 1930.

163. Loading the barge *Russell* with cement at Murston Quay in 1930.

164. Smeed Dean's barge yard at Murston, *c.*1920. The barge in the foreground is probably the *Russell*.

165. The same view in 1956. By this time the yard was used for the maintenance of A.P.C.M. lighters. In the foreground is the derelict barge *Thomas and Frances*.

166. The last barge built by Smeed Dean was the *Youngarth*, seen here at Murston soon after her commissioning in 1913. She was named after Garth Doubleday, the young son of one of the firm's officials.

167. In the heyday of Milton Creek, a barge launch drew great public interest. This is the *Olive May*, the biggest spritsail barge ever built (and the only one built with an auxiliary engine), being launched from Wills and Packham's yard in 1920.

168. Launch of the *Raybel* from Wills and Packham's yard, 1920.

169. In the heyday of barge-building in Milton Creek, two local firms made the ironwork for the barges. They were Littlewood on Milton Hill, and R. Gardiner of the East Kent Ironworks in Frederick Street. This is an advertising photograph for the latter firm's brail winches. Both Robert Gardiner Senior and Junior ran the firm and they are buried together alongside the old mortuary/chapel in Sittingbourne cemetery. Robert Junior was so keen on his barge work that he served on the committee of the Medway Sailing Barge Match prior to his death in 1907. The foundry buildings were later occupied by Medway Fabrications Ltd., but have recently been demolished.

170. The Sittingbourne Shipbuilding Company was established in about 1925 and took over the former White's Yard. They later moved to the larger ex-Wills and Packham yard. The *Trilby* and *Verona* are seen here in Milton Creek for barge-yard work, *c.*1949. The work performed on *Trilby* was a miracle of barge-building – she was lengthened, broadened, deepened and motorised!

171. Some of the local junior sports clubs appeared earlier in this book. The town's main sports team, Sittingbourne F.C., should not be neglected. Formed in 1886 from the ashes of the earlier Sittingbourne United F.C., the club was for long periods one of the most powerful teams in Kent. Home crowds of 3,000 or more spectators were common in the heyday. This photograph shows the Sittingbourne F.C. 1st team (Kent League) squad, wearing the club colours of black and red, after winning the Kent Senior Cup in 1902. Left to right: back row (standing), F. Chandler, F. Lines, R. G. Jarrett, J. Macey, E. J. Garner; middle row (seated), E. G. White, H. Buckland, A. M. Plummer, J. Lodder, E. Garside; front row (on ground), L. B. Grant, T. Cleaver. Local jeweller E. F. Handcock (who later became a club official) sold this picture in the form of a small badge.

172. The Sittingbourne F.C. 1st team (Southern League) squad which won the Kent Senior Cup in 1930. Left to right: back row (standing), McGovern, Johnson, Hillen, Bailey, Coupland, Cook, Cox; front row (seated), Crawford, Potter, Kingsley, Dickie, Swindell, E. Woolven. Centre-half and Captain Bill Dickie joined Sittingbourne in August 1922 (after Football League service with Chelsea and Stoke City) and played on for almost nine seasons. This was the Club's most successful period ever; they appeared in the final of the Kent Senior Cup five times, won it twice (1929 and 1930), and also won several other trophies. The players in this photograph were identified by right-back Hillen in 1981, when he was the only surviving and traceable member of the squad.

173. A momentous occasion in the history of Sittingbourne F.C. These are the Past v. Present teams which played on the Bull Ground to commemorate the 50th anniversary of the Club in 1936. The result was fittingly a 2-2 draw. The Past players are wearing black and red, the Present are in light blue. Left to right: back row, Owen, Sutch, Ridge, Plum, Francis; middle row, Cox, Kingsley, Lukehurst, Dickie, Wilson, Gilgun, Mallett, Burgess; front row, Major, Barney, McLeod, Phillips, Smy, Simms, Pearce, Hambrook, Montgomerie. Identification of the players was made by by L. Lukehurst and W. McLeod.

174. Lloyd's F.C., *c.*1937. At this time they were a powerful Kent League side and their games against the Sittingbourne town club were always great local events, drawing big crowds. Players (from left to right): back row, standing, O'Neill, Kingsnorth, House, Hammond, Hillen, Mason; front row, seated, Smith, Hopper, White, Sellens, Kemp, Fallon, Black. The players were identified by T. Kingsworth, J. Parks and V. Wood.

175. A scene on the Bull Ground in 1894 showing Sittingbourne (in their change strip of white) playing at home to Chatham Town.